D0772262

Poet's Workshop

Read, Recite, and Write

HAIKU

An old silent pond...
frog jumps into the pond,
Splash! Silence again.

JoAnn Early Macken

Dedication
Arthur stands serene
As an oak in summer sun
But his thoughts cat-quick

Author
JoAnn Early Macken

Publishing plan research and development
Reagan Miller

Project coordinator
Kelly Spence

Editor
Anastasia Suen

Proofreader and indexer
Wendy Scavuzzo

Design
Margaret Amy Salter

Photo research
Margaret Amy Salter

Prepress technician
Margaret Amy Salter

Print and production coordinator
Margaret Amy Salter

Photographs and illustrations
All images by Shutterstock

JoAnn Early Macken is the author of *Write a Poem Step by Step* (Earlybird Press), five picture books, and 125 nonfiction books for young readers. Her poems appear in several children's magazines and anthologies. JoAnn has taught writing at four Wisconsin colleges. She speaks about poetry and writing to students, teachers, and adult writers at schools, libraries, and conferences. You can visit her website at www.joannmacken.com.

Library and Archives Canada Cataloguing in Publication
Macken, JoAnn Early, 1953-, author
      Read, recite, and write Haiku / JoAnn Early Macken.

(Poet's workshop)
Includes index.
Issued in print and electronic formats.
ISBN 978-0-7787-1964-9 (bound).--ISBN 978-0-7787-1968-7 (pbk.).--
ISBN 978-1-4271-7602-8 (pdf).--ISBN 978-1-4271-7598-4 (html)

      1. Haiku--Juvenile literature. 2. Haiku--Authorship--
Juvenile literature. I. Title. II. Title: Haiku. III. Series: Macken,
JoAnn Early, 1953- . Poet's workshop.

PL729.M33 2015   j808.1'41   C2014-908196-0
                                           C2014-908197-9

Library of Congress Cataloging-in-Publication Data
Macken, JoAnn Early, 1953-
   Read, recite, and write haiku / JoAnn Early Macken.
      pages cm -- (Poet's workshop)
   Includes index.
   ISBN 978-0-7787-1964-9 (reinforced library binding : alk. paper)
-- ISBN 978-0-7787-1968-7 (pbk. : alk. paper) -- ISBN 978-1-4271-
7602-8 (electronic pdf : alk. paper) -- ISBN 978-1-4271-7598-4
(electronic html : alk. paper)
   1. Haiku--Authorship--Juvenile literature. I. Title.

PN1414.M33 2015
808.1'41--dc23
                              2014046861

Crabtree Publishing Company

Printed in Canada / 042015 / EF20150224

www.crabtreebooks.com 1-800-387-7650

Published in Canada
Crabtree Publishing
616 Welland Ave.
St. Catharines, Ontario
L2M 5V6

Published in the United States
Crabtree Publishing
PMB 59051
350 Fifth Avenue, 59th Floor
New York, New York 10118

Published in the United Kingdom
Crabtree Publishing
Maritime House
Basin Road North, Hove
BN41 1WR

Published in Australia
Crabtree Publishing
3 Charles Street
Coburg North
VIC 3058

Contents

Chapter 1: What Is a Haiku?

A *haiku* is a short poem. This poetic form began in Japan hundreds of years ago. Haiku can mean one poem or many.

Haiku do not have titles. They focus on nature. They include a *kigo*, or season word, to show the time of year. They focus on here and now. That focus shows that everything changes over time.

The first haiku poets used a certain number of sounds, or beats, in each line. This is the traditional pattern:

In many haiku, a **pivot**, or twist, occurs between two of the lines. Read on for more details about haiku.

Line 1 has five beats.

Line 2 has seven beats.

Line 3 has five beats.

Some poets follow this pattern in English. But English **syllables** are not the same as Japanese sounds. Many poets who write in English do not count syllables. They just keep the lines short.

Most haiku have three lines. The middle line is a bit longer. Some haiku have two or four lines. Because haiku are so short, every word counts!

Prose vs. Drama vs. Poetry

In literature, we use different names to talk about the way words are used. As you can see in the examples below, the same story can be told in many different ways.

Prose

When the cherry trees bloom, people meet in the fields. They admire the blossoms. Everyone is friendly.

Drama

TIME: spring
PLACE: city field
STAGE DIRECTIONS: [People meet near blooming cherry trees]
SPEAKER 1: How lovely!
SPEAKER 2: What a beautiful sight!

Poetry

in the city fields
contemplating cherry-trees . . .
strangers are like friends

—Issa

We use sentences to tell a story in **prose**. When a story is performed as a play, it is called a **drama**. Can you see the stage directions? They let the actors know when and where things happen.

The third example is a **poem**. A poem uses short **phrases**, or groups of words, to tell a story or share a feeling.

Writing Your Own Haiku

Haiku show respect for nature. When you write haiku, start with nature. Remember that nature is everywhere, even in cities. If you need ideas, take a walk outside. Or remember a moment that moved you. Think about what you notice at a certain time of year. Use all of your senses. What can you hear, see, smell, taste, and feel? Use these words to describe the season.

You can use the 5-7-5 syllable pattern if you want to. You might find that you like the challenge. It might help you use as few words as possible. Either way, try to keep your lines short.

Haiku use images to show feelings. Use specific words to paint a clear picture. An image can also be a **symbol** of a season. Cherry trees are a symbol of spring in Japan. Mentioning cherry trees tells the reader that the poem takes place in spring.

Whatever you choose, write about it as though it is happening right now. Even if you write about a memory, write as though it is happening here and now.

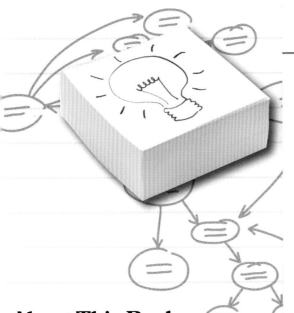

About This Book

In this book, you'll learn about one type of poem: the haiku.

Literature Links explore the tools that all types of literature use.

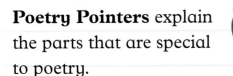

Poetry Pointers explain the parts that are special to poetry.

Thinking Aloud sections include discussion questions, brainstorming tips, graphic organizers, and examples of students' writing.

Now It's Your Turn! gives you tips on how to write your very own haiku.

Five Steps to Writing

1. Pre-writing: Brainstorm new ideas. Write every one down, even if it seems as though it might not work.

2. Drafting: Your first copy can be sloppy. You can always fix it later.

3. Revising: Use input from other writers to make your poem better.

4. Editing: Check spelling, grammar, and punctuation.

5. Publishing: Print and distribute your poem, give it as a gift, or publish it online.

Chapter 2: Writing a Sound Haiku

Listen. What do you hear? In this chapter, you will read, recite, and write a sound haiku. To start, think of something that makes a sound.

crossing it alone
in cold moonlight...the brittle bridge
echoes my footsteps

Taigi

the laden wagon runs
bumbling and creaking down the road...
three peonies tremble

Buson

Compare the two poems. In the first one, footsteps echo. In the second, a wagon creaks.

What sound could you write about?

Poetry Pointer: Compression

Suppose you spill a glass of juice. You grab a napkin and wipe it up. When you squeeze the juice out of the napkin, you **compress** it. To compress means to squeeze. You can do the same thing to a poem. You can squeeze out any extra words. When you write haiku, use as few words as possible. Cut empty words such as *very, suddenly, quite, only, really, even,* and *just.* Can you cut out *a* or *the*? Look at this sentence:

The snow falls on the trees.

Try it!

To use fewer words, you could say this instead:

 Snow falls on the trees.

Or you could paint an even clearer picture. Use an adjective instead of an article.

 Snow falls on bare trees.

Finally, you don't even have to write in full sentences. Use **fragments** instead.

snow on bare trees

Literature Link: Present Tense

To make your haiku sound as though it is happening now, use verbs in the present **tense.** Here are some examples of verbs in present and past tense:

present tense	past tense	present tense	past tense
I echo	I echoed	I hop	I hopped
you echo	you echoed	you hop	you hopped
he, she, or it echoes	he, she, or it echoed	he, she, or it hops	he, she, or it hopped

Thinking Aloud

Where do sounds come from? People talk, hum, and recite poetry. They tap, stomp, and snap their fingers. Animals grunt, howl, and peep. Doors slam. Windows rattle. Machines whir and click. Nature has its own sound effects. Wind, waves, and hail all make sounds.

Each season can have its own sounds. Brett's group made a chart of sounds they heard in different seasons.

spring	summer	fall	winter
robin chirping	sprinklers	leaves rustling	ice cracking
thunder	bees buzzing	geese honking	snow plows
melt water dripping	swimmers splashing	football games	carolers singing
baseball games	lawnmowers	leaf blowers	furnaces
	motor boats		
	fans		

What do you hear at different times of the year?

Write Your Own Sound Haiku

Brett heard an owl hoot one winter night. It seemed to be asking a question. He listened for an answer. He wrote about the sounds in his poem.

> Late night Q and A—
> two owls hoot out in the cold.
> Where are you? I'm here!

Now It's Your Turn!

Choose a sound from the students' chart or think up your own. What do you hear around you? Does your house rattle? Does a refrigerator hum? Do you hear someone snoring at night? Try to include a season word. The house could rattle in a spring storm. Maybe the snorer is wrapped in a thick quilt.

> Think of animal sounds if you want. Maybe you hear spring peepers. Maybe bees buzz. Maybe the snorer is a bear in a cave!

What do you hear in your classroom?

Do sounds change over the course of a school year? How?

What activities change?

Does bad weather ever keep you indoors?

Do students take part in annual events?

Is school ever canceled because of bad weather?

What happens in your neighborhood?

What do you hear?

Chapter 3: Writing a Change Haiku

From day to day, we grow and change. Things around us change, too. We change our minds. Our moods change. In this chapter, you will read, recite, and write a haiku about change. The first poem describes a poet's change of mood. The second poet finds a surprise.

angry I strode home . . .
but stooping in my garden
calm old willow-tree

Ryota

Hi! My little hut
is newly-thatched I see . . .
blue morning-glories

Issa

What else changes over time? Think about what is different than it used to be.

Poetry Pointer: Turning Points
Many haiku contain a twist or change between two of the lines. In the first poem, that twist occurs between lines 1 and 2. The speaker is angry in line 1. In line 2, the person sees something calming. Do you think the speaker changes?

In the second poem, the turning point lands between lines 2 and 3. A little hut is transformed overnight. The change takes place between the lines.

The **contrast** between two images is part of what makes a haiku a haiku. An angry person contrasts with a calm, old tree. Blue morning glories change a hut's roof. See if you can create two images that contrast with each other.

Literature Link: Conventions

Conventions are like rules, or the way things are usually done. They tell you when to add a period or a comma. They remind you to begin a sentence with a capital letter.

Haiku use little or no punctuation. Line breaks can take its place. But you can use it if you want to. Use it only where you think it is needed. Punctuation often fits at the turning point. You could use a dash, a comma, a colon, an exclamation point, or a question mark.

When you write poetry, you can bend the rules. You can decide whether to use punctuation. You can use capital letters where you think they are needed. Just make your poem easy to understand.

Thinking Aloud

Fashion changes every year. Medicine leaps forward. Communication keeps improving. What else can you think of that changes? You can use a chart to help you brainstorm. Divide it into sections that make sense to you. Add ideas in each section. Colin's group thought of four kinds of things that change. They listed people, animals, places, and things.

people

- grow
- learn
- get haircuts
- travel
- move
- make new friends
- graduate
- change schools

animals

- grow
- transform
- migrate
- molt
- build nests
- raise young

places

- city buildings are built
- islands pop up
- forests grow
- crops are planted and harvested
- wind shapes mountains
- rivers change course
- glaciers melt

things

- flowers open and wilt
- cars, planes, trains move
- roads, bridges, houses are constructed
- clothes get dirty and clean again
- water freezes
- ice melts
- chemicals react
- food cooks

14

Write Your Own Change Haiku

One summer, Colin watched a monarch caterpillar change. He saw it hatch from a tiny egg. It munched on milkweed leaves. As it grew, it **molted**, or shed its skin, five times. Then it turned into a butterfly and flew away! He wrote about the process in his haiku.

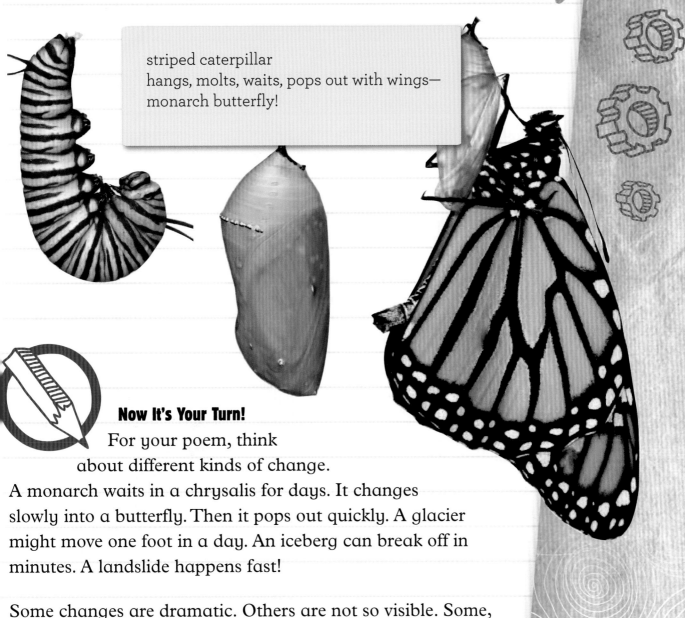

striped caterpillar
hangs, molts, waits, pops out with wings—
monarch butterfly!

Now It's Your Turn!

For your poem, think about different kinds of change. A monarch waits in a chrysalis for days. It changes slowly into a butterfly. Then it pops out quickly. A glacier might move one foot in a day. An iceberg can break off in minutes. A landslide happens fast!

Some changes are dramatic. Others are not so visible. Some, like our feelings, are inside us. Have you ever waited on pins and needles for a test score? How did the result affect your mood? What does the last day of the school year feel like? What kind of change will you write about?

Chapter 4: Writing a Weather Haiku

The weather is a wonderful source of ideas for poets. It changes from day to day. It can be cool or warm, wet or dry, stormy or calm. Skies might be sunny one minute and cloudy the next. In this chapter, you will read, recite, and write a haiku about weather.

These poems both feature rain. What is the same? What is different?

windy winter rain . . .
my silly big umbrella
tries walking backward

Shisei-Jo

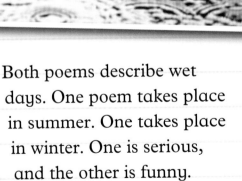

mirror-pond of stars . . .
suddenly a summer shower
dimples the water

Sora

Both poems describe wet days. One poem takes place in summer. One takes place in winter. One is serious, and the other is funny.

You can take any number of approaches to a poem. Weather has many options. What kinds of weather have you seen? What kinds have you heard or read about? What kinds of weather will you write about?

When you write, make the best choice for every word. How do you decide which words are best?

Meaning is the most important factor. Be as specific as possible. Use a dictionary to find out what words mean.

A **thesaurus** can give you lists of **synonyms**, or words that mean almost the same thing. For example, leap, hop, and jump all mean about the same thing.

Words with similar meanings might sound very different. One might be a better fit with the language of your poem.

Another word may be a better fit for the **tone**, or the feeling or emotion, of your poem.

One word might fit the **rhythm** of your poem better than another word with the same meaning.

When you write haiku, look for words that fit the season. Use words that describe the weather. Think about these season hints:

- What clothes do people wear?
- How do trees and plants look?
- How do animals behave?

Literature Link: Personification

In the second poem, the poet writes about an umbrella as though it is alive. It tries to walk backward on its own. This is called **personification**.

You can do the same thing. You can write about a nonliving object as though it is alive. You can also write about an animal or object as though it is a person.

> Could your desk stand up and walk away?

> Use your imagination!

> Could a pencil dance?

> Could a book turn its own pages?

Thinking Aloud

Jenni's group looked up weather words in a thesaurus. They used a chart to list the words they found.

sky	wind	precipitation	temperature	storms
sunny	gust	pour	chilly	cloudburst
clear	blast	drizzle	blazing	tempest
calm	gale	rain cats and	frigid	blizzard
cloudy	blustery	dogs	tropical	squall
overcast	breeze	snow	sweltering	turbulent
	brisk	rain	torrid	raging
	draft	sleet	fiery	wild
	puff	hail	roasting	rough
	zephyr	fog	scorcher	
		mist	balmy	

Write Your Own Weather Haiku

Jenni wrote about a blustery day. She used personification in her haiku. She imagined her scarf coming alive.

> scarf flies from my neck
> tickles the fence with its fringe
> hugs a leafless tree

Jenni also hinted at the season. A scarf with fringe suggests cold weather. She used *leafless* to show that the season is fall or winter. What words could she have used to show a different season?

spring: buds
summer: leaves
winter: snow

You can think about other options.

Now It's Your Turn!

Now write your own weather haiku. Feel free to use the weather words in the group's chart. You can also add more of your own. Use a thesaurus if you like.

Use personification if you want. What might come alive in your poem? What kind of weather will you write about?

Chapter 5: Writing a Question Haiku

Are you curious? Do you wonder about things around you? In this chapter, you will read, recite, and write a haiku with a question in it. If you want, you can include the answer, too. This example does:

One fallen flower
returning to the branch? . . . Oh no!
A white butterfly

Moritake

Sometimes a closer look gives us an answer!

Poetry Pointer: Counting Syllables

Many haiku are translated from other languages. The translator must make a choice. How important is counting the syllables? Shouldn't the focus be on the meaning? Of course, the meaning matters more.

Most haiku have three lines. Some have two or four. The meaning of the words counts more than the syllables.

Count the syllables in the example. Line 2 has eight. The translator must have thought that each word was important enough to keep. When you write, you can choose, too. You can count 5-7-5. You can stick to the tradition or skip it. Just keep the lines short.

Literature Link: Alliteration

Two words in the first line of the poem start with the same sound. *Fallen flower* is an example of **alliteration**. This kind of repetition is a pleasant pattern to hear in a poem. You can use it, too!

You might have a choice between two words that mean about the same. Choose the one with the beginning sound that matches a nearby word.

You can look in a thesaurus for synonyms. Choose one with the sound you like.

Here are more examples of alliteration:

loud, lilting laugh

burst a bunch of balloons

quiet, curving cul-de-sac

Remember that the sound is what matters, not the spelling. In the third example, the words start with *q* and *c*. What matters is that they share the beginning *k* sound.

21

Thinking Aloud

The students in Luke's group thought about questions and answers. They wondered. They daydreamed. They made a list of things they wanted to know.

What color is a tree frog?

How does a cricket chirp?

Do bats hibernate?

Where do mushrooms grow?

Who invented toothpaste?

Does anything live on the moon?

What would you like to know? If you want to find an answer, you can use a KWL Chart.

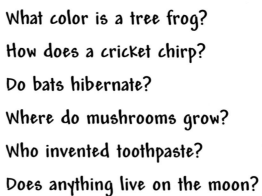

What I Know	What I Want to Know	What I Learned
Crickets chirp	How does a cricket chirp?	Only the male cricket chirps. It rubs a sharp edge on one wing against ridges on the other wing.

Start with what you know. Write it in the "What I Know" column. Under "What I Want to Know," ask your question. Then do your research. Add what you found out to "What I Learned." You can use the words in your chart to write your poem.

Write Your Own Question Haiku

In spring, Luke helped his family plant a garden. All summer, he helped care for it. He watered and weeded. He staked up droopy plants. In fall, he helped pick vegetables. He wondered about the seeds he had planted. Here is his poem:

> How does a tiny seed
> hold the green winding secret
> of this pumpkin vine?

Now It's Your Turn!

What are you curious about? Do you ever wonder about other places? What is life like on the other side of the world? What does a volcano sound like? How does a rain forest smell? What grows in a desert? What does an astronaut feel in space?

Maybe your question has no answer yet. You don't need to find an answer to write your poem. A good question can be enough.

23

Chapter 6: Writing a Direct Address Haiku

An address can be a number on a street. It can be a string of letters that send email to someone's inbox. It can also be a speech.

In the United States, President Abraham Lincoln gave an important speech in 1863. He spoke in Gettysburg, Pennsylvania. He said that all people are equal. That speech is called the Gettysburg Address.

A poem of direct address speaks directly to someone or something. In this chapter, you will read, recite, and write a direct address haiku.

Each of these poems speaks to something.

I must turn over . . .
beware of local earthquakes
bedfellow cricket!

Issa

swallow in the dusk . . .
spare my little buzzing friends
among the flowers

Basho

The first poem is a gentle warning. The second one is a plea. How else do the two poems differ? How are they alike?

Poetry Pointer: Apostrophe

Speaking to the subject of a poem is called **apostrophe**. A poem of direct address is also called an apostrophe poem. To write your poem, decide who or what you would like to speak to. Then think about what to say.

Literature Link: Point of View

Who will speak in your poem? That voice shows the **point of view**.

> First person: The speaker in the poem uses *I, me,* or *we.*

Second person: An apostrophe poem uses this point of view. (So do our two examples.) The speaker in the poem speaks to someone or something. It can use *you,* either singular or plural.

Unless you are trying to show two different perspectives, the point of view should stay the same for the whole poem.

Third person: The speaker in the poem talks about someone or something. It uses *he, she, it,* or *they.* (That's everyone except *you* and *me.*)

25

Thinking Aloud

Zoe's group thought about who or what they might like to speak to. They brainstormed some types of people, places, and things.

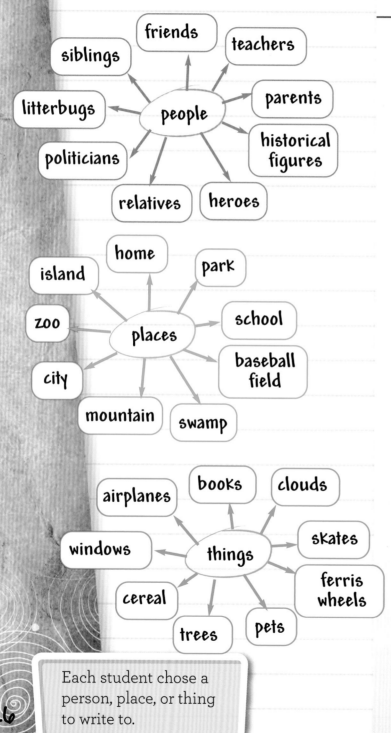

friends
siblings
teachers
litterbugs
people
parents
politicians
historical figures
relatives
heroes

home
island
park
zoo
places
school
city
baseball field
mountain
swamp

books
clouds
airplanes
things
skates
windows
ferris wheels
cereal
trees
pets

Each student chose a person, place, or thing to write to.

Then they thought about what to say. They listed these ideas:

Ask a computer for help.

Tell a tree you wish it well.

Thank a wind farm for trying.

Complain to an alarm clock.

Tell the planet you care.

Praise a pet.

Scold a litterbug.

Ask a textbook for an answer.

Tell your classroom what makes it cozy.

Ask a baseball field for luck.

Tell a parent about a problem.

Tell your notebook what you think of homework.

Write Your Own Direct Address Haiku

Zoe's family visits Lake Michigan every summer. They stroll on the beach. They wade in the water and search for shells. Her family also feeds the sea gulls. Zoe wrote a **thanku**, a combination of haiku and a thank you note. You can do that, too! Here is Zoe's first draft:

Dear Lake Michigan,
your calm waves give me comfort
every single day

Now It's Your Turn!

Now choose who or what you will speak to in your poem. What do you have to say? Your poem does not have to be thankful. It might be funny instead. It can be thoughtful. It can even be angry. It can show any feeling you feel. Write about something you care about. Your poem will be stronger if you write about a subject that stirs up an emotion.

In the next chapter, you can see how Zoe's group helped her revise her poem.

You can choose from the students' idea list. You can think up your own ideas. Write to a person, place, or thing.

Chapter 7: Revising Your Haiku

Congratulations! You have just completed the first two steps of writing. You brainstormed new ideas. You used them to write your first draft. Now you are ready for the next two steps: revising and editing. Use this checklist as a guide:

Yes/No	Revision Checklist
	Does your haiku include one or two clear images?
	Does your haiku use present tense?
	Have you used season words?
	Could you cut any extra words?
	Did you include a turning point or twist?

Group Help

One good way to revise your poem is to share it with a group. Give each person a copy. Ask them to write their comments on it. Ask one person to read your poem aloud. Listen for any places where the reader stumbles. Give the others a chance to speak before you say anything about your work.

Then move to the next writing step. Did they see anything you need to edit? Are there any errors in spelling, grammar, or punctuation?

Take time to think about every comment. Try the ideas that make the most sense to you.

Zoe's group liked her idea of writing to the lake. Brett thought she should add a season word. Colin suggested changing *calm* to *cool*.

Zoe agreed. "That means summer," she said. "Most of the year, the water is freezing!"

Jenni said, "You could change *give me comfort* to *comfort me*. That would cut one word."

Luke reminded Zoe that she should use present tense. She changed the last line to be more specific.

Here is Zoe's revised poem. She counted the syllables and decided she liked it this way.

Dear Lake Michigan,
your cool waves comfort me
on this awful day

Helping others revise and edit their poems can help you, too. When you read others' work, look for the positive. Point out what works well. Be supportive. Writing is not easy, and sharing can be even harder! If you don't understand something, ask a question.

Chapter 8: Performing a Poem

A *haiga* combines haiku with art. The traditional form includes a painting and a poem. The poem is written in **calligraphy**, or decorative handwriting. The painting is simple, with only a few lines and colors. The poem fits the art but does not have to explain it. Newer haiga might use photos.

After you write your haiku, make a haiga. Paint or draw a simple background. Or choose a photo that fits the season. Print your haiku in a simple font by hand or on a computer. Make a poster of your haiga to hang on a wall. Or create a slideshow with your classmates.

Practice reading your poem aloud.

Speak slowly.

Speak clearly.

Read with feeling.

When you are ready, have a haiga party. Invite others to see your work. Show the art. Give visitors a chance to study your work. Then read the poems aloud. Listen when others read. Share the haiga joy!

Learning More

Books

The Cuckoo's Haiku and Other Birding Poems by Michael J. Rosen.
Candlewick Press (2009)
Guyku: A Year of Haiku for Boys by Bob Raczka.
HMH Books for Young Readers (2010)
Haiku: Learn to express yourself by writing poetry in the Japanese tradition by
Patricia Donegan. Tuttle Publishing (2003)
Hi, Koo!: A Year of Seasons by Jon J Muth. Scholastic Press (2014)
Write a Poem Step by Step by JoAnn Early Macken. Earlybird Press (2012)

Websites

Haiku:
www.pbs.org/parents/creativity/ideas/haiku.html
Build a haiku from available words. Fill in the 5-7-5 blank lines.

How do you write a haiku?
http://web-japan.org/kidsweb/explore/language/q2.html
Haiku: World's Shortest Form of Poetry, Part 1:
http://web-japan.org/kidsweb/cool/12-12/index.html
Haiku: World's Shortest Form of Poetry, Part 1:
http://web-japan.org/kidsweb/cool/12-12/002.html

Poetry Idea Engine
http://teacher.scholastic.com/writewit/poetry/flash_pie.htm
(Press "play," then click on the blue waves to create a haiku.)

Glossary

Note: Some boldfaced words are defined where they appear in the book.

alliteration A series of words that begin with the same sound

contrast A comparison between two things that are not alike

fragment An incomplete sentence

point of view The speaker's position in relation to a poem or story

rhythm A pattern of regular sounds in a series of words

syllable One of the parts into which a word is divided when it is pronounced

symbol An object that stands for something else

tense The form of a verb that shows time as past, present, or future

thanku A combination of haiku and a Thank You note

thesaurus A book with lists of words that have similar meanings

Index